Professional Speaking Profitability

Turning Your Expertise into a Lucrative Platform

Table of Contents

Chapter 1. Introduction

Unleash the power of your knowledge and skill with our comprehensive Special Report on "Professional Speaking Profitability: Turning Your Expertise into a Lucrative Platform." Packaged with alluring positivity and excitement, this non-technical guide will take you on an intriguing journey of exploring how you can transform your professional expertise into a bountiful speaking career. Our charmingly penned report will motivate you, educate you, and guide you as you venture into the world of professional public speaking. From strategies in building your brand, identifying lucrative opportunities, to captivating and retaining your audience, this Special Report is designed to boost your confidence, increase your professional visibility, and unlock your potential for significant profitability. Are you ready to dive in and step onto the stage of success? This report is your waiting backstage pass! Secure your copy today and let's turn that spotlight on you!

Chapter 2. Unveiling the Power of Professional Speaking

The world of professional speaking offers endless opportunities, especially for those who possess specific and advanced knowledge or skills in a particular field. This arena of public and often persuasive presentation not only allows you thorough exploration of your specialty and its perspectives but also aids in consolidating your knowledge, increasing your professional visibility, establishing credibility, and yes, transforming this process into a lucrative vocation. No doubt, it is an entrancing entrepreneurial venture, but to make the most out of it, one should be well-acquainted with the associated challenges and how to overcome them.

2.1. Venturing into the World of Speaking

You have the knowledge, the skills – but how do you thrust yourself into the spotlight of the professional speaking world? To do so, it's essential to understand what the profession involves. Despite its intricacies and nuances, the underlying framework remains quite simple — expert individuals sharing their knowledge to inform, inspire, and influence.

Starting your journey in this profession requires proficiency in conveying your expertise in a clear, concise, and compelling manner. While fear of public speaking is normal, even for seasoned professionals, overcoming this obstacle can unlock a trove of opportunities, engagement, and impacts that simply cannot be achieved elsewhere.

2.2. Building your Brand

The first integral part of this journey towards soaring profitability is to ensue and evolve a robust personal brand. Your brand is essentially the persona that you present to the world, and it should encapsulate your unique skills, experiences, and the message you want to share. It should also reflect your values; these act as guidelines shaping your professional decisions and ensure consistency in how you present yourself.

How do you establish a personal brand that resonates with your potential audience? First, obviously, gain clarity in what you want to project. Is it technical knowledge? Practical wisdom? Or perhaps a combination? Then, ensure the consistency of this entity across your public profiles and engagements. This uniformity instills trust and affinity, making it easier for potential clients or audiences to resonate with you.

2.3. Fostering Audience Connection

Connecting with your audience is pivotal in professional speaking, as it directly influences the impact of your presentation and your perceived credibility. Ideally, each member should feel directly addressed and personally engaged by your presentation.

Developing a deep understanding of your target audience can help create this connection. What are their interests, their preferences, their challenges, and how does your expertise address these? Without this essential knowledge, even the most intricately designed presentations could fail to make an impact.

2.4. Finding Lucrative Opportunities

Once you've built a solid brand and have honed your skills to connect with an audience effectively, it's time to identify and seize lucrative opportunities. These could be speaking engagements at industry conferences, guest lectures at educational institutions, or corporate training sessions.

To locate these opportunities, leverage your existing network, attend industry-specific events, and ensure your professional social media profiles reflect your speaker persona. Proactively approaching organizations and event organizers with a clear and concise proposal highlighting your expertise and value proposition can also yield positive results.

2.5. Speaking that Sells

To ensure sustained success in this field, you need to develop the skill of speaking that sells. Your primary objective might not be to sell a product or a service, but each speaking engagement is essentially an opportunity to sell your brand, your ideas, and your expertise.

Taking control of the stage with confidence, impacting thousands while subtly persuading them towards your viewpoints, that's where the magic lies. Yes, impart information, but don't starve your audience of the experience of your personality and distinctive perspectives. Make each presentation a seamless blend of knowledge, stories, experiences, and enthusiasm.

To unlock the power of professional speaking, dive into the world of your audience, understand their needs and preferences, and create content that resonates with them. Build a solid brand to represent your unique expertise and deliver every talk with confidence, clarity, and something extra — a piece of yourself. Let the spotlight on the stage shine on not just the professional speaker, but the passionate individual who stands behind the knowledge.

In taking these steps, professional speaking profitability is not just a vision but an achievable reality. The journey might be challenging initially, but with perseverance and continuous learning, the power and profitability in this market can undoubtedly be yours.

Chapter 3. Understanding Your Expertise: A Self-Assessment

There's a buzzword often thrown around in the world of personal development and career progression - expertise. But what does it mean? Essentially, your expertise is the unique intersection of your knowledge, skills, and experience. It's what sets you apart and makes you a sought-after commodity on the professional speaking circuit. However, before we can package and sell that expertise, we need to understand it fully. This involves a deep and introspective journey of self-assessment.

3.1. The Power of Introspection

Self-assessment is a vital first step on your journey to professional speaking profitability. This analysis requires you to dive deep and explore your abilities, experience, and unique insights. It's not just about listing your skills on paper. It's about analyzing the core of who you are, what you believe, and what value you bring to the world.

A good self-assessment should consider both hard skills and soft skills. Hard Skills are your technical skills and competencies you've gained over your career. Soft skills, on the other hand, involve emotions and intuition. They are about how you interact with others, make decisions, and approach your work.

3.2. Identifying Your Hard Skills

Your hard skills are easiest to identify. They are often the skills you've learned and honed over the years through education, work experience, and professional training. Whether you're an engineer, an artist, a CEO, these skills are your ticket to entry in your field.

To put together a list of your hard skills, consider the following categories:

1. Formal education: Degrees, qualifications, and certifications.
2. Professional experience: Skills you've obtained from past jobs.
3. Ongoing professional development: Conferences, workshops, online courses.
4. Technical skills: Proficiency in software, programming languages, or other tools.

3.3. Identifying Your Soft Skills

Soft skills, on the other hand, might seem harder to pinpoint. These revolve around your personality, your approach to problem-solving, and how you work in a team. Communication, leadership, resilience, adaptability, and empathy are examples of these integral skills.

To identify your soft skills, think about how you interact with others, how you manage stress, how you handle criticism or failure, and how you motivate and inspire those around you. Reflection, seeking feedback from peers, mentors, and past performance reviews can be helpful in identifying these.

3.4. Uncovering Your Unique Selling Proposition

Once you have articulated your hard skills and soft skills, it's time to uncover your unique selling proposition (USP). Your USP is the unique combination of skills, experiences, and personality traits that distinguish you from other speakers on the circuit.

To identify your USP, consider:

1. Your unique combination of hard skills and soft skills.

2. Success stories: Times in your career when your unique mix of skills and experiences led to outstanding results.

3. Your passions and values: these can often add a unique edge to your expertise.

The inclusion of your passions and values into your USP not only makes your offering more authentic but also increases the likelihood that you'll attract an audience that resonates with your message.

3.5. Skills Gap Analysis

Once you've identified your current skills and USP, the next step in understanding your expertise is to analyze any skill gaps. These are areas in which further development could enhance your marketability as a speaker.

Comprehensive skill gap analysis should incorporate the following steps:

1. Identify the skills most highlighted by successful professional speakers.

2. Compare these with your own skillset.

3. Identify areas for development or upskilling.

Remember that attaining new skills can be transformative, but also consider refining and mastering the skills you already possess.

3.6. Conclusion

A deep understanding of your expertise is a crucial foundation for a profitable speaking career. By turning this given reflection into action, you will not only amplify your strengths but also address any areas of improvement. This self-assessment is your launching pad to success, where value, uniqueness, and continuously sharpening your skills converge to create an unstoppable trajectory towards your career as a professional speaker. Let this be the prelude to your symphony of success.

Chapter 4. Preparing Your Unique Pitch: Building a Compelling Narrative

Every effective presentation begins with a narrative, a story that's distinctively yours. Your unique pitch is not merely a sequence of data points, but an engaging story that unites your experiences, knowledge, and audience's interests. Crafting a compelling narrative is essential in delivering an impactful insight into your personal journey and expertise.

4.1. Understand Your Unique Offering

In the world of public speaking, the mantra "be yourself" must be your guiding light. To distinguish yourself, you need to understand what makes you unique. Is it your teaching style? Is it your profound industry knowledge? Or maybe it's your ability to inspire others with your personal experiences? Once you've identified your unique attributes, they should form the basis of your narrative.

Each professional speaker has their own unique blend of attributes to offer. Write down your attributes, chart your professional experiences, and map out the knowledge you've gained throughout your career. This personal and professional inventory serves as the foundation on which your unique pitch is based.

4.2. Create An Emotional Arc

Narrative structure is a crucial aspect of any successful pitch. In essence, an emotional arc is a sequence where you lead your audience through a set of emotions to the ultimate end—a changed perspective, a shift in knowledge, or a new challenge to face. Script it from your listener's perspective and analyze how they might react at different phases.

Start with framing your problem or challenge. Describe the landscape before you began your journey to induce empathy and connection. Then transition to the steps you took, decisions you made, or insights you had that led you to where you are now. Use emotional highs and lows to generate intrigue and suspense. Ultimately conclude with an answer to the problem, a resolution to the question, a way out of the challenge.

Every powerful narrative has a fulcrum or a turning point. Identify yours and anchor your narrative around it.

4.3. Test and Refine

Now that you've built your narrative's framework, it's time to test, refine, and polish it for a wider audience. You might find some parts need trimming while others require amplification. Phase it in a way that hooks your audience from the get-go and keeps them engaged throughout.

Draft your pitch, then evaluate. Remove anything that doesn't serve your story or makes it difficult to follow. This might be excess information, confusing details, or anything irrelevant to your narrative.

Remember, refining your pitch involves - simplifying complex ideas, adding a touch of personal experiences, including anecdotes to support your arguments, and ensuring the underpinning message remains clear.

4.4. Practice Makes Perfect

Once your pitch is finalized, rehearse it. Practice is the secret sauce that transforms a good narrative into an extraordinary one. It isn't just about memorizing words: it is going beyond the lines to connect with your message emotionally.

During your practice sessions, pay attention to your body language and diction as well. Use your voice and physical expression to add depth and bring your narrative to life. Remember, your narrative is only as good as how well you deliver it.

Repetition will lead you to discover viewpoints or segments of your narrative that can be improved. You'll also get familiar with your flow, and flexibly adapt if you are distracted or interrupted during your actual presentation.

4.5. Get Feedback

Consider conducting a few dry-runs in front of a supportive yet objective audience, someone who can provide constructive feedback about your pitch - what worked, what didn't, and areas you could improve upon.

This could be a mentor, a colleague, or even a family member. Take their feedback into consideration. Let it help you refine your pitch, improve your delivery, and ultimately build a more compelling narrative.

4.6. Enjoy the Process

Finally, while it might seem like a long journey, creating a compelling narrative should be enjoyable. You're delving into your past, addressing your challenges, and sharing your wisdom with others. So why not enjoy it?

Take your time, discover facets about yourself that you may have overlooked, add a touch of humor, and make it a story worth sharing. Remember, your audience can tell when you're excited about your story. Enthusiasm is infectious!

In conclusion, building a compelling narrative for your pitch is about authenticity, structure, precision, practice, and feedback. An engaging narrative resonates with audiences, making you a favored speaker. With time, you'll find that each presentation adds a new chapter to your narrative, enriching it even further. And that's what transforms you from just another speaker to a storyteller, from professional expertise to a lucrative platform.

Chapter 5. Establishing Your Personal Brand: The Foundation of Profitability

In the realm of professional public speaking, your personal brand stands as the cornerstone on which all other structures of your career are built upon. It is the foundation of profitability, as it enables you to make a lasting impression, define your unique selling proposition, and carve out a distinguished space in a saturated market.

Let's delve deep into this process of establishing your personal brand for a profitable speaking career.

5.1. Identifying Your Unique Selling Proposition

In order to establish a strong brand, you need to start with identifying your unique selling proposition (USP). This part of your brand highlights your unique qualities or features that differentiate you from other speakers. A compelling USP convinces your potential clients the exact value you're bringing to the table.

Perhaps it is your unmatched expertise in a specific area, your ability to deliver complex ideas in a digestible and engaging way, your humor, or your compelling personal journey. What's pertinent is to identify this USP and hone it in such a way that it instantly catches the attention of your audience and potential clients.

5.2. Building Your Personal Narrative

Your personal narrative forms the core part of your personal brand. It authenticates your USP and helps create a strong emotional bond with your audience. Your personal story, your journey of challenges, triumphs, lessons, and growth – these are the elements that resonate with your audience at a personal level.

To create a strong personal narrative, begin by jotting down the essential elements and experiences of your life that have shaped you and your viewpoint of the world. Carefully weave these elements into your narrative in such a manner that empathetically conveys your persona and passion to your audience.

5.3. Consistent Brand Image

In order to establish an enduring brand in the market, consistency is key. Create a brand image that consistently resonates with all your marketing materials, messages, and even your appearances. This consistency should be evident in your website, social media profiles, your presentations, and all other public outlets.

Develop a unique and consistent visual brand identity that includes your logo, color scheme, fonts, and style, which mirror the personality and values that your brand stands for.

5.4. Cultivating Trust and Credibility

Trust is a crucial element of your brand. It determines whether your potential clients are motivated to hire you or whether your audience is willing to listen to you. To cultivate a trustworthy brand image, integrity should be an inherent quality of all your actions.

Your credibility is often judged by your qualifications, experiences, past performances, testimonials, and your association with reputable organizations. Make it a point to highlight your accomplishments and proofs of your competence.

Speaking engagements, webinars, authoring books, writing articles, appearing as a guest expert on popular media channels, and being a part of professional associations are some effective ways to build your credibility.

5.5. Personal Brand Visibility

Once you've built your personal brand, the next step is to make it visible to the world. Use content marketing strategies to share valuable insights, ideas, and experiences that resonate with your brand and audience.

Join online forums, attend events and conferences, network with industry leaders and enthusiasts, share your expertise on various platforms, and adopt an effective social media strategy.

5.6. Auditing Your Personal Brand

Just like any other aspect of your business, your personal brand, too, requires regular audits. Consistently evaluate your brand's performance. Assess how your brand is being perceived by your audience and whether it is resonating with your USP and values. Make necessary tweaks and adjustments based on this feedback.

Your personal brand is an extension of who you are and what you offer. It is the mirror that reflects your persona, your expertise, and your values to the world. The process of building your brand can seem intimidating and complex, but remember, your brand is your story. And just like any story, it develops and takes shape with time. So take the first step, start weaving your narrative, and watch how your personal brand begins to bloom and grow.

Chapter 6. Strategies for Securing Lucrative Speaking Engagements

In today's fast-paced world, public speaking is more than just standing up on stage and delivering a speech. It's an art that requires strategic planning, research, and honest self-evaluation. In order to secure lucrative speaking engagements, you must stand out in a crowded market, deliver incredible value, and know your audience inside and out.

6.1. Understand Your Unique Selling Point

The first step in securing lucrative speaking engagements is understanding your unique selling point (USP). Your USP is what differentiates you from the countless other speakers clamoring for attention.

Do an honest self-evaluation and identify your strengths. Do you excel in motivational speeches? Are you an expert in a specific field? Do you have a unique combination of skills that can help solve problems for your audience? Or perhaps you have a compelling personal story? Once you have identified these strengths, build your brand around your USP.

Remember, your USP is not just about you. It is about the value you bring to your audience. The more you can help solve problems or help your audience achieve their potential, the more lucrative your speaking engagements will be.

6.2. Build an Influential Network

One crucial aspect of securing speaking engagements is networking. Building an influential network takes time and effort, but it is often the fastest route to securing lucrative speaking engagements.

Don't just network to sell – network to collaborate. Attend industry conferences and events and engage with thought leaders and influencers in your field. Connect with event organizers, booking agents, and other professionals who can potentially offer you speaking engagements.

Remember that networking is about building relationships, not just exchanging business cards. Show genuine interest in what others are doing and offer help where you can. The deeper the relationship, the more likely you are to be considered when opportunities arise.

6.3. Leverage Online Platforms

In today's digital era, virtual speaking has become a lucrative opportunity for many professionals. Webinars, online courses, and virtual conferences are all opportunities for you to showcase your expertise and connect with a global audience.

Develop your online presence by consistently creating valuable content and engaging with your audience on social media platforms. Leverage LinkedIn, a platform specifically designed for professionals, to share your insights, join relevant groups, and connect with potential clients.

Additionally, consider creating your own website. This not only gives you a professional image but also provides a platform for sharing blogs, videos, and other forms of content that demonstrate your expertise. It doubles up as a portfolio showcasing your previous speaking engagements, client testimonials, and the value you have provided to your audience.

6.4. Master Proposal Writing

A well-written proposal can be your ticket to lucrative speaking opportunities. Be clear about the objectives of your speech, the value you will deliver, and how it aligns with the purpose of the event.

Remember, event organizers are looking for speakers who can add value to their event. Point out how your topic is unique, timely, and relevant to their attendees. The more unique and valuable your proposal, the higher the likelihood of it being accepted.

Your proposal should also include your speaking fees. Be sure to benchmark your fees based on your speaking experience, expertise, and the market rate.

6.5. Continuously Improve your Skills

As a professional speaker, you must have a relentless commitment to excellence. Continuously hone your presenting skills, improve your stage presence, and master the art of storytelling. It's also important to keep updating your content to keep up with trends and relevant topics.

Prospective clients will judge you based on your past performances. Remember, word of mouth matters in this industry. A stellar performance can lead to more bookings, while anything less could leave you struggling for opportunities.

6.6. Negotiate Strategically

When offered speaking engagements, negotiation is an invaluable skill. Understand your value and don't be afraid to ask for what you're worth. Be prepared to explain why your fee is justified and remember, your negotiation power increases as your professional reputation grows.

In conclusion, securing lucrative speaking engagements is not about chance. It's about leveraging your unique talents, building influential relationships, establishing a professional online presence, mastering proposal writing, improving your speaking skills, and negotiating effectively. With these strategies, you'll be well-positioned not only to secure speaking engagements but also to make them immensely profitable.

Chapter 7. Presentation Techniques: Captivating and Engaging Your Audience

Audiences come to presentations with the expectation of gaining something new and valuable. How you deliver your content determines whether you capture or lose their attention. Here, we explore key techniques that will help you captivate and engage your audience.

7.1. Understanding Your Audience

The fundamental rule for engaging any audience is knowing who they are. Think of the audience as the target for your message. Who are they? What are their interests? Understanding this helps you craft a presentation that resonates with them. When designing your presentation, consider:

1. Demographics: Age, profession, education, background all contribute to our worldviews and perspectives. An audience of baby boomers will perceive your message differently from a millennial audience.

2. Prior knowledge: Know what your audience already understands about your topic. This way, you can build on existing knowledge and avoid alienating them with too simple or too complex content.

3. Expectations: Realize what they hope to gain from your presentation. Ensure your objectives align with their expectations.

By acknowledging these factors, you foster a connection with your audience, making your message more impactful.

7.2. Crafting Compelling Stories

Anecdotes and stories capture attention and make presentations relatable. They simplify complex information, making it more digestible for the audience. You can craft your stories by:

1. Building a Narrative Arc: Every good story follows a sequence - a beginning, middle, and end. Your beginning should introduce the premise, the middle explores the premise, and the ending provides a satisfying resolution.

2. Relating to the Audience: Make sure your stories resonate with their experiences. This establishes an emotional connection, and emotional connections are powerful engagement tools.

3. Incorporating Humor: When used appropriately, humor can break barriers and cultivate a relaxed atmosphere. However, it's essential to use humor sensibly – you don't want to risk offending your audience.

7.3. Visual Aids: The Power of Show and Tell

Visual aids supplement your verbal communication, each enhancing the other. Here are some ideas:

1. Use Slides: Slides with key points, graphs, and visuals can add variety to your presentation and help your audience retain information better.

2. Body language: Your non-verbal cues like gestures, eye contact, and facial expressions play a key role in maintaining audience engagement.

Remember, though, your visual aids should not become a crutch. They are there to support your message, not distract from it.

7.4. Interactivity: Involve your Audience

Active participation makes your audience feel valued and helps keep them attentive. You can cultivate interactivity by:

1. Asking Questions: Regularly posing questions encourages participation and keeps the audience stimulated.

2. Conduct Quick Surveys: Tools like live polling can gather instant feedback, making your audience feel involved.

Interactivity creates a two-way dialogue, fostering a more engaged audience.

7.5. Valuing Time and Keeping Pace

Respect your audience's time. Prepare your content to fit the allocated time, and stick to it. Conversely, pace your presentation to neither rush nor drag. A steady pace maintains audience attention throughout.

7.6. Rehearse, Rehearse, Rehearse

Rehearsing boosts confidence, allowing you to deliver your content smoothly. Practice in front of a mirror, record yourself and review, or solicit feedback from friends and family.

Following these strategies can help transform your presentations, making them captivating and interactive; an invitation for your audiences to truly engage with your content.

Chapter 8. Maximizing Event Aftermath: Capitalizing on Engagement and Feedback

In the modern age of public speaking and professional expertise, it's critical to capitalize on both audience engagement and feedback. This crucial process begins immediately after the event itself, leveraging your hard-earned platform to solidify connections, optimize future presentations, and of course, maximize profits.

8.1. Transforming Engagement into Lasting Relationships

After every speaking event, a flurry of engagement ensues. This golden opportunity could come as business card exchanges, LinkedIn connection requests, or further collaboration queries. Each of these interactions cultivates a potential seed for enduring professional relationships.

Take intentional steps to nurture these relationships soon after making first contact. Follow up with personalized messages, thanking each individual for their interest and time. It might seem rudimentary, but this courteous and professional approach reveals a lot about your character and brand giving you an upper hand in cultivating relationships.

Remember, in a digital age, your online presence becomes your brand ambassador. Regularly update your professional profiles, such as LinkedIn, and maintain an active, engaging presence on social channels.

8.2. Cultivating Feedback for Continuous Improvement

Feedback is the most reliable compass that directs our path to self-improvement. Portfolio never remains constant; it evolves through continuous refinement shaped by constructive feedback.

Post-event surveys work wonders in acquiring comprehensive feedback. Apart from gathering individual audience analysis such as "how was the talk?" or "rate the speaker," also focus on in-depth insights like "what could be improved?" and "what additional topics are you interested in?" These views allow for both a macro and micro view at understanding your audience better.

Handling criticism is also part of the process. Not all feedback will be favorable, but every piece is valuable since it comes straight from your audience's perspective. If taken constructively, even negative feedback paves new paths towards positive alterations and growth.

8.3. Tailoring Content Based on Audience Response

There is an unequivocal relationship between your speaking material and the audience's response. A seemingly brilliant piece might fail to resonate, while an off-the-cuff story could turn out to be a favorite.

To capture your audience's preferences, monitor and analyze the reactions. Which parts of your talk sparked the most questions, what led to a myriad of 'aha moments', or conversely, which parts lost your audience's attention?

Study these cues post-event, as they are direct indicators of what engages and what bores your audience. This examination will assist in tailoring your content, delivery style, and reinforce your connection with the audience for any future interactions.

8.4. Leveraging Testimonials to Boost Visibility

There is no better endorsement than the one coming from satisfied audience members. A simple review can provide a vast amount of credibility to your professional profile.

To capitalize on this, request attendees to leave testimonials or reviews post-event. You might facilitate this process by providing a streamlined platform, such as a Google form or an email template, to submit these reviews.

Once collected, these testimonials become an indispensable part of your portfolio. Display them on your website, or share them on social media. Remember to ask for permission before publicizing these testimonies, though; respectful professional conduct goes a long way.

8.5. Seizing Opportunities: The Art of Follow-ups

Follow-ups are a potent tool to translate a one-time engagement into a long-term connection, or even collaborations.

The successful strategy here is not to explicitly 'sell' but to sincerely engage in communication that reinforces your brand personality. Follow-up messages should be brief but compelling, personalized but professional, and always express gratitude for the previous cooperation.

Endeavor to facilitate a dialogue rather than a monologue. Instead of incessantly talking about your merits, ask them questions, show genuine interest in their work, and explore possible opportunities to collaborate.

Whether a fellowship, a business venture, or another speaking opportunity, this smart networking expands your professional horizons and potentially skyrockets your profitability.

Indeed, event aftermath is an intensive period filled with rich prospects. By strategically capitalizing on engagement and feedback, you can forge enduring connections, continuously improve your content, and enhance your professional and economic growth. Step confidently into this phase, knowing that every experience and every contact is another stepping stone towards public speaking success.

Chapter 9. Long-Term Success: Building Resilience and Adaptability in Your Speaking Career

Professional speaking, like any entrepreneurial pursuit, requires a solid foundation alongside flexibility and the capacity to adapt in the continuously shifting landscape of this field. An invincible blend of resilience and adaptability can take you a long way into a thriving and rewarding career in professional speaking. But what does it really mean to be resilient and adaptable? How can we cultivate such qualities? Let's delve deeper.

9.1. Building Resilience

Resilience isn't just about surviving challenges; it's about thriving despite them. It's about constantly moving forward, picking yourself up when you fall, and learning from your experiences. In the realm of professional speaking, resilience can take many forms.

First, let's discuss managing rejection. The path to professional speaking success isn't going to be one smooth journey. You'll likely face rejection multiple times - from event organizers, potential clients, or audiences who weren't moved by your words. That, however, isn't something to be disheartened by. As a professional speaker, you need to understand that rejection is a part and parcel of your journey. Embrace each NO as an opportunity to learn and grow. Dealing with rejection equips you with increased resilience and teaches you not to take things personally.

Furthermore, being resilient requires mastering your mind. You need to cultivate a growth mentality that views challenges as opportunities rather than obstacles. The right mindset focuses on potential, experimentation, growth, and perseverance. A resilient mind filters out the negative, absorbs the positive and uses setbacks as stepping stones to greater heights.

9.2. Cultivating Adaptability

Just like resilience, adaptability is also a critical attribute that aids in long-term success in your speaking career. It means responding to changing circumstances with ease and flexibility, without losing sight of your overarching goals.

Every audience is different and every event unique. As a speaker, you need to be able to gauge the mood and expectations of your audience, and anticipate their needs. Adaptability allows for more versatile and engaging presentations. It enables you to tweak your message to resonate with each specific audience, therefore leading to more impactful outcomes.

Moreover, adaptability involves keeping pace with the evolving trends of the speaking industry. For instance, the shift towards digital platforms and virtual events, driven by technological advancements and, more recently, by the COVID-19 pandemic. Adapting to new modalities and tools can aid in expanding your reach and effectiveness as a speaker.

9.3. A Resilient and Adaptable Approach to Speaking Opportunities

At an operational level, staying resilient and adaptable means looking for opportunities in unconventional areas. Perhaps there's a local community event that needs a keynote speaker or a virtual conference on a topic you're passionate about. Seize opportunities wherever they present themselves, even if it means moving out of your comfort zone.

Additionally, take up gigs that may not pay as much but offer exposure to a different, potentially larger, audience. Such resilience in seeking opportunities and adaptability in content delivery can open up new avenues and create growth momentum over time.

Resilience and adaptability also come into play when increasing your professional visibility. How do you respond to feedback, both positive and negative? Can you convert criticism into opportunities for self-improvement? Can you seamlessly adapt your brand image and communication methods to different platforms and demographics?

9.4. Remaining Resilient and Adaptable Over Time

As your journey as a professional speaker evolves over time, you'll have to consistently nurture and practice resilience and adaptability. Engage in regular self-assessment and feedback sessions to understand where you stand and where you are heading. Stay agile and be prepared to pivot as per the current demand and trends of the speaking industry.

Most importantly, be persistent. Not every speech will attain the intended results. Not every audience will connect with your talks. Each hiccup, each setback is an opportunity to learn and bounce back stronger. By cultivating resilience and adaptability, you're not only empowering yourself but also setting the stage for longevity and prosperity in your professional speaking career.

Remember, the path of professional speaking is a marathon, not a sprint. With resilience and adaptability as your steadfast companions, you're equipped to navigate the undulating terrains of this exciting journey and reach the pinnacle of long-term success in your career!

Chapter 10. Business Models and Revenue Streams in Professional Speaking

The path to profitability as a professional speaker is closely linked to your chosen business model and the revenue streams it encapsulates. There is not a one-size-fits-all approach. Your choice of business model can significantly influence your income, the growth of your brand, and your speaking career's sustainability. Let's embark on this journey, begin to understand, adapt, and act.

10.1. Understanding Business Models in Professional Speaking

A business model delineates how your professional speaking business creates, delivers, and captures value. One of the biggest mistakes you can make when entering this field is assuming that paid speaking events are the sole revenue stream. As a professional speaker, be ready to turn every stone — paid speaking, writing, consulting, and training. Diversifying your revenue streams not only maximizes your earnings but also ensures a more stable income.

10.2. Popular Business Models

Below are some of the popular business models in professional speaking:

1. The Paid Keynote Speaking: This model focuses primarily on delivering keynotes for a fee at conferences, seminars, corporate events, and educational institutions.

2. The Seminar Leader: In this model, the speaker hosts seminars or

workshops, either independently or through partnerships with other organizations.

3. The Training and Development Speaker: Besides giving talks, these speakers offer tailored training and development courses to companies or individuals.

4. The Coach/Consultant: As a coach or consultant, the speaker leverages their subject matter expertise by providing guidance on a one-on-one basis or to a company.

5. The Hybrid: This model is a combination of the above models and often involves providing additional value-added services such as writing books or creating online courses, along with speaking.

Assess the audience you are trying to reach, your speaking style, and your long-term goals while deciding your business model.

10.3. Key Revenue Streams in Professional Speaking

Talking about business models is incomplete without investigating the underlying revenue streams. Therefore, let's explore them:

1. Speaking Fees: The most direct revenue stream is the fee charged for giving talks. The fee varies depending upon experience, reputation, demand, and negotiation skill.

2. Product Sales: Many speakers create products like books, DVDs, or online courses. The sale of these products represents a significant revenue stream.

3. Consulting Fees: If you're an expert in a particular area, you can charge consulting fees for providing expert advice.

4. Trainings: Charged either per participant or on a per-session basis, this income source can be extremely lucrative, particularly for in-demand subjects.

5. Retainers: For speakers who offer ongoing services, especially coaches or consultants, a retainer can serve as a regular and predictable income source.

6. Commissions: Partnerships with other businesses or affiliates where you earn a commission on every referral or product sale.

10.4. Optimizing Income Opportunities: The 360° Approach

Despite the importance of diversification, you need to remember that not all revenue streams are equal. Some will likely be more profitable than others, depending on factors such as your area of expertise, your target audience, and market trends. The key is to adopt a 360° approach, focusing equally on the quality of your service and efficiency of income generation. However, don't spread yourself too thin. Remember, expertise takes time!

10.5. The Business Model Canvas: A Tool for Success

The Business Model Canvas, devised by Alexander Osterwalder, is an excellent tool to map, discuss, design, and invent new business models. The canvas visibly projects how you create, deliver, and capture value, putting emphasis on your value proposition, customers, channels, customer relationships, revenue streams, key resources, key activities, key partnerships, and cost structure. It can clarify how to optimize your revenue streams and business model.

10.6. Adapting with Agility: A Note on Resilience

The professional speaking industry is not immune to changes.

Technological evolutions, societal changes, or economic climate shifts impact its dynamics. The ability to be agile and adapt your business model and revenue streams consequently can make or break your career. Remain open to change, keep learning, and, most importantly, don't let failures deter you. Instead, use them to rise stronger.

While business models and revenue streams form the financial backbone of your professional speaking pursuit, placing the audience at the core of your venture should remain your ultimate guide. Remember, it's about making a positive impact on others through your words. That's where the magic of professional speaking truly lies.

Chapter 11. The Future of Professional Speaking: Trends and Opportunities

The world of professional speaking is evolving at a surprisingly swift pace. What used to be a field dominated by those with celebrity status or decades-long careers in a niche market has transformed into a dynamic industry attracting diverse speakers from numerous professions and walks of life. The future of professional speaking is not just for a select few anymore. It's a growing industry with opportunities for anyone with a unique message and the passion to share it.

11.1. Emergence of Virtual Platforms

As the world is moved by the relentless pace of technological evolution, so too is the professional speaking industry. An important trend is the rise of virtual platforms for speaking. As digital technology becomes even more integrated into our everyday lives, professional speakers are finding new ways to connect with their audience. Virtual platforms offer not only geographical flexibility but also the convenience of tailored interactions.

Webinars, podcasts, YouTube channels, and platforms like TED Talks have emerged as popular virtual platforms for professional speaking. These platforms have democratized knowledge sharing by providing a platform for anyone with an internet connection to learn, share, and engage on a global scale. The ability to broadcast your message to millions of viewers all around the world greatly expands the scope of professional speaking opportunities.

As a professional speaker, there are several ways to harness the power of virtual platforms. You can host webinars or online workshops on topics related to your areas of expertise. Podcasts can be used to share insights and experiences with a wider audience. Meanwhile, video platforms such as YouTube and TED Talks allow you to share your ideas visually and interactively, providing a more intimate and compelling way to engage with your viewers.

11.2. Changing Audience Preferences

The preferences of the audience are changing at a rapid pace. The new age audience values authentic and relatable content more than ever. Anyone with a compelling story, a unique viewpoint or specialty, can generate a following. Pivoting to these changing trends, professional speakers are altering their speaking styles. Interactivity, personalization, and digital engagement have emerged as key drivers in delivering substantial and meaningful messages.

For professional speakers, staying relevant thus entails a vigilant comprehension of the audience's evolving preferences. It runs the gamut from integrating personal anecdotes into your speeches to imparting real, actionable instructions. Adopting a conversational tone, incorporating humour and triggering thought-provoking discussions are becoming increasingly pivotal in the speakers' efforts to maintain audience engagement.

However, the evolving audience preferences also entail challenges. Striking a balance between meeting their expectations and staying true to your style might be tough, yet it is critical. The right tone, content, and delivery can result in a powerful synergy that not only captivates your audience but creates memorable experiences.

11.3. Evolution of Content

As the demand for professional speakers grows, so too does the demand for specific content. Traditionally, professional speaking engagements focused on motivational or leadership topics. Now, there is a growing interest in a wider range of material, including subjects related to sustainability, mental health, diversity and inclusion, technology, and more.

In addition, audiences increasingly yearn for bespoke and actionable content. They desire presentations that offer not just theories but practicable tools and strategies that they can implement in their lives or in their respective business operations. Speakers who are adept at delivering such content tend to garner significant attention and demand.

The future of professional speaking entails an even greater shift toward niche specialization, with audiences seeking expertise and insights on increasingly focused topics. This means that having deep knowledge in a particular niche and the skill to translate this knowledge into engaging and accessible speech content will be increasingly valued.

11.4. Expanding Opportunities for Monetization

The future of professional speaking is also set to witness a significant boom in opportunities for monetization. Cross-pollination of skills where professional speakers double as coaches, authors, consultants, or trainers is on the rise. By diversifying their income streams, professional speakers are able to capitalize on their skills, offering a range of services to meet the needs of their increasingly diverse audience.

That said, a word of caution is in order for anyone intending to penetrate these ancillary avenues of monetization. While multiple revenue streams increase the potential for income, it is vital to ensure that the quality of your core offering, namely your speaking engagement, is not compromised.

To effectively balance expanding monetization opportunities with maintaining the quality of your core speaking services, a strategic approach will likely be necessary. This can involve outsourcing non-core activities, proper scheduling to prevent overcommitment, and regular skill enhancement to ensure that you remain at the top of your game across all your income streams.

11.5. Increased Access to Training and Resources

With the growth of the professional speaking industry comes an abundance of resources. New speakers are fortunate to have access to a wealth of training programs, mentorship opportunities, and various resources to hone their speaking skills. Speakers' associations offer professional development programs, networking events, continuing education, certified speaking professional (CSP) credentials, and access to research and publications in an effort to support their members.

In the future, the increased access to professional speaking resources is anticipated to spike and subsequently deliver more refined and adept speakers. The improved quality of speakers will, in turn, fuel the evolution of the professional speaking landscape even further, making it a self-perpetuating cycle of growth and development.

In conclusion, the future of professional speaking is indeed an unfolding panorama of boundless opportunities. With an emerging shift towards virtual platforms, evolving audience preferences, and expanding opportunities for monetization, this landscape is ripe for exploration by fresh and established speakers alike. By observing these trends and positioning yourself at the forefront of these shifts, you stand a good chance of turning your expertise into a dramatically profitable speaking career.

41

www.ingramcontent.com/pod-product-compliance
Lightning Source LLC
Chambersburg PA
CBHW071017260726
48661CB00007B/3003